30 L
DE

LORD, TEACH US TO *Pray*

LESTER ELLIOTT

EVERFAITH PRESS

2013 EverFaith Press Edition

Lord Teach Us To Pray/ Elliott, Lester

ISBN: 9781937844110

Library of Congress Control Number: 2013942356

Ellechor Media, LLC
EverFaith Press
1915 NW Amberglen Pkwy, Suite 400
Beaverton, OR 97006

Printed in the United States of America.

www.everfaithpress.com

DEDICATION

To my precious wife Erma Rhonda who
has encouraged and inspired me over
the years.

To our loving sons and their wives who
give so much joy to our lives:
Lee and Shruti
Raoul and Donna
Donny and Tiffany

ABOUT THE AUTHOR

Lester Elliott is the senior pastor of the Lauderhill Seventh-day Adventist Church. He has been in ministry for over 37 years, including 5 years as a hospital chaplain. Lester holds a Master of Divinity degree and training in Chaplaincy. He has pastored in England, Trinidad and Tobago, New York, Michigan and now in Florida.

CONTENTS

INTRODUCTION

WHILE ATTENDING COLLEGE, a friend, who was a much more brilliant student than I was, startled me with these words, "Lester, do you know you do not need to pray? If you can do something, there's no need to pray." My friend and I were of the same faith, and we had attended church school together, but somehow he concluded that prayer was not a necessity. I responded in anger, "You are a fool!" I later apologized for this outburst, but my friend's statement was suggesting that prayer was for the weak or those who lacked self-confidence. I had no good answer to share with him at the time, and his statement haunted me over the years. It has since been my quest to understand the reason for and meaning of prayer.

Prayer is a common feature of many human cultures. Every belief system has the practice of prayer embedded in it. Jews, Hindus, Muslims, Buddhists, and Christians all pray.

Although prayer is so commonplace, there is much misunderstanding about what it is and how it works. Some people chant repetitive words, some just hum a sound, some pray through saints or ancestors, and others pray directly to God.

But is there any real value in prayer? Why pray at all? Is prayer just an exercise we engage in to make us feel better about ourselves? Is it just a psychological game...or can we truly communicate with a superior being?

Jesus taught and demonstrated through His life that communication with God through prayer is real. He taught that prayer is the privilege of all—anyone can pray if he or she chooses. Prayer can transform your life and bring out the best in you. Prayer is for your benefit.

This little book is the result of my daily devotions and the thoughts I entered into my journal as I reflected on each passage. I was amazed and inspired, and I hope you will be too, as you reflect on these lessons and take your journey with Jesus through His prayer life.

After most chapters, there are three questions for reflection which are intended to help you meditate on what you have read. This can be done individually or in a group. I have also concluded each chapter with a sample prayer that should help inspire you in your own prayers after you have reviewed each lesson. As you grasp the key concepts of what a focused prayer life looks like—a real, daily communion with your heavenly Father, prayer will become an exciting experience for you, and you will soon discover how essential it is in your daily living.

My prayer is that you will be blessed and transformed as you engage in communion, conversation and fellowship—with Jesus our Savior, our heavenly Father, and the Holy Spirit as you pray.

Lord, teach us to pray.

Lesson 1

PRAYER: A CALL TO BE LIKE GOD, PART I

Matthew 5:43-47

"You have heard that it was said, 'Love your neighbor and hate your enemy.' But I tell you, love your enemies and pray for those who persecute you, that you may be children of your Father in heaven. He causes His sun to rise on the evil and the good, and sends rain on the righteous and the unrighteous. If you love those who love you, what reward will you get? Are not even the tax collectors doing that? And if you greet only your own people, what are you doing more than others? Do not even pagans do that?"

In His first teachings at the beginning of His ministry, Jesus outlined the principles of His kingdom. Featured prominently was the principle of *prayer*.

The first thing Jesus revealed about prayer is that it is

not a selfish act—*it is a magnanimous and generous act.* "Pray for those who persecute you."

Prayer is a call to be like God who cares for His enemies. "He causes His sun to rise on the evil and the good, and sends rain on the righteous and on the unrighteous" (Matthew 5:45). God is gracious, generous, forgiving, and redeeming. When we pray, we are seeking to be like Him.

How unfortunate and sad, then, that we pray so little for those who do us wrong! How disappointing that many Christians today demonstrate hatred toward those who do not believe as they do. They seek the power of government to pass and enforce laws to compel conformity with their beliefs, and some use explosive language to incite hatred against those whose beliefs and actions they do not approve. This is quite evident in the issues that dominate our political and social discussions today, like same-sex marriage, contraceptive coverage in healthcare insurance, abortion, undocumented immigrants, and Muslim extremists. Much of the discourse reveals hate, not love.

True prayer is a call to live a more noble life than simply "loving your neighbor and hating your enemy." "Even sinners do that," Jesus said. To hate is to live a life that is no better than that of a person who does not know God. Loving only those who love you brings no lasting reward and certainly no approval from heaven.

Prayer calls you to resist the temptation to persecute those who seek to do you harm. It is a call to do the more noble deed, to love as your Father in heaven does. Prayer, therefore, serves as a reminder that your persecutor or enemy, or anyone who is different from you, is your brother or sister and that he or she needs your love. Love is the only power that can change the human heart. "God is love" (1 John 4:8), and through prayer we receive the power of His love that transforms us.

Jesus defines the children of His Father as those who pray for their enemies. Our Lord is teaching that we cannot sincerely pray for someone *and* hate them at the same time. Prayer transforms the one who prays. It softens his heart and gives him strength and courage to respond to his enemy with love. Jesus calls this "perfection," when we love as our Father in heaven loves.

A life of prayer, therefore, is a call to live in the atmosphere of heaven instead of the pollution of this sinful and evil world of hate.

What a high standard of living Jesus reveals in His first public message!

Questions for Reflection

1) How does Jesus describe or define the children of His Father?

2) How does God respond to those who are evil?

3) How can we be perfect as our Father in heaven is perfect?

Prayer

Heavenly Father, teach me to love as You do. Give me of Your grace that I may love, forgive, and pray for those who do me wrong. Remove from my heart the tendency to ridicule or even hate those whose beliefs are different from mine. Help me to reflect Your loving heart of forgiveness and grace always, for I am Your child and You are my Father. Amen.

Lesson 2

PRAYER: A CALL TO BE LIKE GOD, PART 2

Luke 6:27-36

"But to you who are listening I say: Love your enemies, do good to those who hate you, bless those who curse you, pray for those who mistreat you. If someone slaps you on one cheek, turn to them the other also. If someone takes your coat, do not withhold your shirt from them. Give to everyone who asks you, and if anyone takes what belongs to you, do not demand it back. Do to others as you would have them do to you."If you love those who love you, what credit is that to you? Even sinners love those who love them. And if you do good to those who are good to you, what credit is that to you? Even sinners do that. And if you lend to those from whom you expect repayment, what credit is that to you? Even sinners lend to sinners, expecting to be repaid in full. But love your enemies, do good to them, and lend to them without expecting to get anything back. Then your reward will be great, and you will be

children of the Most High, because He is kind to the ungrateful and wicked. Be merciful, just as your Father is merciful."

IT WOULD SEEM that Jesus said more in His first teaching on prayer than Matthew recorded. Luke, after his careful investigation, added more details to the message of Jesus.

Prayer should change the behavior of a person from one who strikes back when wronged to one who turns the other cheek, from one who is vindictive to one who forgives. The praying Christian does not seek to repay evil with evil; he learns that only light can transform darkness and only love can cure hate. Prayer makes the follower of Jesus generous. Instead of prosecuting one who steals from him, he does the unthinkable: he offers him what was stolen as a gift. This is totally foreign to what most societies, and human nature, demands. A life of prayer, therefore, is a call to live on the high plane of grace and mercy rather than the level of "an eye for an eye."

Achieving this standard of living does not happen overnight. True prayer demonstrates a daily submission to the control of a merciful God who showers His blessings on the good and the evil, on the righteous and the unrighteous. A person who truly prays will neither be violent nor be unjust. He would do to others as he would have them do to him.

From the above Scripture, we learn that prayer also helps us to become concerned about the less fortunate in society and to lend without expecting repayment. In other words, we become generous. True generosity reaches beyond those whom we may believe to be good and deserving—it reaches to our enemies, too. Jesus taught that we should do to our enemies what they do not expect: shower them with love and mercy.

The reward of the praying Christian reaches beyond this world. His or her reward is greater than any earthly possession. He or she becomes a son or daughter of the Most High God. Our lives will reflect the perfect life of the one true God who is kind to the ungrateful and the wicked. The praying Christian becomes merciful just as his or her heavenly Father is merciful. This is how we live a heavenly life in a sinful world.

Questions for Reflection

1) How can we overcome the natural desire to retaliate when we are wronged?

2) What actions should accompany our prayers for those in need?

3) Is there any benefit in praying if we do not desire to be more generous and gracious as our heavenly Father is?

Prayer

Lord, thank You for caring about all Your children, the good and the evil. Make me more like You. Grant that my prayer will reflect my actions. Give me a generous and forgiving attitude that I may reflect who You are. Help me to be merciful as You, my heavenly Father, is merciful. This I pray, in the name of Jesus my Savior. Amen.

LESSON 3

PRAYER IS NOT A PERFORMANCE

MATTHEW 6:5-15

"And when you pray, do not be like the hypocrites, for they love to pray standing in the synagogues and on the street corners to be seen by others. Truly I tell you, they have received their reward in full. But when you pray, go into your room, close the door and pray to your Father, who is unseen. Then your Father, who sees what is done in secret, will reward you. And when you pray, do not keep on babbling like pagans, for they think they will be heard because of their many words. Do not be like them, for your Father knows what you need before you ask him.

"This, then, is how you should pray:

'Our Father in heaven,
hallowed be your name,
Your kingdom come,
Your will be done,
on earth as it is in heaven.

Give us today our daily bread.
And forgive us our debts,
as we also have forgiven our debtors.
And lead us not into temptation,
but deliver us from the evil one.'

"For if you forgive other people when they sin against you, your heavenly Father will also forgive you. But if you do not forgive others their sins, your Father will not forgive your sins."

JESUS, IN THIS, His first teaching, expands on the principle of prayer. He reveals specifically how the Christian should pray.

First, He lets us know that hypocrites pray, too. Who are hypocrites? Those whose lives do not match their words. They may give the impression that they believe in prayer, but their lives are unchanged. They pray to impress others, and love to pray in public, to be seen. Such praying does not impress God.

Second, Jesus tells us that believers in false gods also pray. They pray long, wordy prayers, but they bring no benefit. In fact, such prayers are not prayed to the one true God; they are empty words offered to gods that can neither hear nor answer.

Jesus is therefore teaching that prayer is not a performance. Prayer is communion, true communication, with our Father in heaven. A prayer that seeks to impress others by its rhetoric is not genuine and will not receive a response from heaven. Its only reward is the praise of those who are impressed.

Prayer, first and foremost, is a private audience with the God of heaven and earth. Public prayer is of no value to a person who has not experienced the privilege of private communion with God. Jesus reveals in this passage that God is not moved by long, showy prayers without meaning. What He seeks is sincerity and genuineness from our hearts when we pray.

God knows what we need before we speak a word. Prayer, therefore, is the submission of one's self to God who already knows everything about us. We do not need to impress Him with words but humbly come before Him, trusting in His mercy and grace.

Jesus next gives what is commonly called "the Lord's Prayer." He taught that prayer must be simple and sincere—not that these words are to be repeated every time we pray! He was giving this prayer as an example, as a pattern of how to pray, representing the elements of genuine prayer.

Genuine prayer, as we see, begins with praise and thanks to the God of heaven, in recognition that He is our Father, a holy God who condescends to listen to us.

Next Jesus taught that we should pray for God's will to be done on earth, in our lives, as His will is done in heaven. We should pray for Him to take back control of this sinful world and establish His promised kingdom, His reign when sin will be destroyed. Prayer develops a longing for a time of peace when God makes all things new.

Genuine prayer, Jesus next shows, focuses on our spiritual wellbeing, our salvation, before our physical needs. If our physical needs supersede our spiritual needs, then we need to refocus. Physical needs are temporary, but our salvation links us to eternity.

God does, however, care about our temporal needs, so He does invite us to place them before Him. Jesus shows us that God promises to supply our needs—though not necessarily all our wants—by revealing that we should ask and thank Him for our "daily bread."

Genuine prayer also seeks forgiveness. It is the recognition that we are sinners, always in need of God's grace. Those who sincerely pray and accept God's forgiveness are so thankful that they in turn seek to forgive those who do them wrong. Prayer is a call to be like our Father in heaven who offers forgiveness to all. You cannot pray sincerely and be left with an unforgiving heart.

This pattern of prayer taught by Jesus ends with an appeal to God for protection. We seek protection from the Devil, deliverance from his schemes to destroy us, and good judgment to avoid his temptations. True prayer recognizes that we are unable to live good lives on our own. We need God's enabling grace. We need a God who watches over us day and night. And He will, when we ask Him to, in prayer.

Questions for Reflection

1) What can we learn from the fact that hypocrites and believers in false gods also pray?

2) Why is sincere prayer more than the recital of words and phrases, even if they are taken from the Bible?

3) For what purpose did Jesus teach His disciples the "Lord's Prayer"?

Prayer

Gracious Father, teach me to come before You with a sincere heart and to present before You my fears and my joys. Give me a thankful heart, a heart that praises You for Your blessings. May Your will be done in my life as Your will is done in heaven. Grant me a forgiving spirit, for You have forgiven me my sins. Thank you for providing for my needs. I trust in Your protection. These blessings I seek in the name of Jesus my Lord. Amen.

BEGIN YOUR DAY WITH PRAYER

MARK 1:35

Very early in the morning, while it was still dark, Jesus got up, left the house and went off to a solitary place, where He prayed.

WHILE ANYTIME IS a good time to pray, it is of extreme importance that we begin each day with prayer. Early in the morning, before the challenges of the day confront us, we should commit ourselves to God our Father. It is best to focus on the holiness of our heavenly Father and His grace that He gives to us generously while the mind is fresh.

Before we are bombarded by the Devil's temptations that can catch us off guard, we can be assured of victory. We can be safe and secure because we began the day with our minds centered on Christ our victorious Lord.

The Holy Spirit is given to those who pray and ask for

Him, and it is a privilege to begin the day with His presence to guide our lives. We can begin each day with His conviction that we, though sinners, are forgiven and given a new beginning as we trust in the grace of Christ. Each day can be started with the assurance that we can, by Christ's enabling grace, live a redeemed and victorious life.

Prayer that is true communion and fellowship with a holy God is private and personal, as is prayer for daily strength and victory. Jesus demonstrated this by leaving His disciples and going to a solitary place, early in the morning, to pray.

Effective prayer is not a display, or for the hearing of others. It is an intimate and private meeting with the God of the universe. God is eager to share one on one time with you. What a blessing!

A prayer life is much more than communal prayers in front of others. Victory and power in the Christian life come primarily from our quiet and private sessions of prayer and meditation. A person who prays publicly but has not had private and personal communion with God has not really prayed at all. Public prayer becomes more meaningful and sincere when bolstered by our personal encounter with God.

Questions for Reflection

1) Why is it best to begin each day in prayerful communion with God?

2) Why did Jesus choose to go apart, in private, early in the morning to pray to His Father?

3) How do we receive victory and power to live the Christian life?

Prayer

Heavenly Father, thank You for the example of Jesus. Give me the desire to spend time alone with You. May Your divine power, the Holy Spirit, come into my life and be my guide, today and every day as I seek You. Help me to follow the example of Jesus and begin each day in communion and fellowship with You. Amen.

Lesson 5

FASTING: NOT A PERFORMANCE BUT AN ACT OF SUBMISSION

Matthew 6:16-18

"When you fast, do not look somber as the hypocrites do, for they disfigure their faces to show men they are fasting. I tell you the truth: they have received their reward in full. But when you fast, put oil on your head and wash your face, so that it will not be obvious to men that you are fasting, but only to your Father, who is unseen; and your Father, who sees what is done in secret, will reward you."

In His first public teaching, Jesus addressed an accepted practice that on some occasions accompanied prayer, the practice of fasting. How the practice started, He did not address, but it is evident that it was common during His time. That He instructed how it should be done suggests that it is a practice that should continue today.

Prominent persons in the Bible fasted. Moses fasted for forty days when he received the Commandments from God on Mount Sinai, and Jesus Himself fasted for forty days after His baptism in preparation for His ministry to save the world. Nations also, in times of deep distress or danger, called on their people to fast.

Fasting is the voluntary abstinence from food for a spiritual purpose. Some may fast for health reasons, but Jesus was addressing fasting from a spiritual standpoint. Fasting makes a person more spiritually sensitive, focusing the mind more on the spiritual than the physical. It is an expression of total dependence on God.

Jesus does not command fasting, however—it is a voluntary act. He simply said, "*When* you fast...." Fasting is a choice, a personal seeking after God.

Just as in the case of prayer, Jesus wants us to know that hypocrites also fast. They fast for show, to impress others. Such fasting becomes a performance in order to appear righteous before others. These acts do not impress God and bring no spiritual benefit to the performer.

When done for the right reason, the seeking after God, however, Jesus says it should be a private act. In fact, fasting should not be obvious to others; it should be a secret between you and God. Look happy when you are fasting! Smile when you fasting! God, who knows everything about you, will respond to your private desires. Jesus is teaching that we cannot impress God either with our prayers or our fasting. These are opportunities to surrender ourselves to the control of a loving God who cares for us and will grant what is best for us.

Genuine fasting also focuses our minds on our spiritual wellbeing, our eternal destiny above our physical and temporary existence. The primary purpose of fasting, therefore, is the sincere reaching out to God and placing complete trust and dependence on Him.

Questions for Reflection

1) Why should fasting not be an opportunity to display before others how righteous we are?

2) How should we appear to others when we fast?

3) What is the primary purpose of fasting?

Prayer

Heavenly Father, You know everything about me. Help me to seek Your presence without pretense. Teach me to seek You always, with a joyful and thankful heart. Thank You for Your promise to bless me according to my needs. Amen.

Lesson 6

THE DEEPER MEANING AND PURPOSE OF PRAYER

Matthew 14:22, 23

Immediately Jesus made the disciples get into the boat and go on ahead of Him to the other side, while He dismissed the crowd. After He had dismissed them, He went up on a mountainside by Himself to pray. When evening came, He was there alone. . . .

Mark 6:46-48

After leaving them, He went up on a mountainside to pray. When evening came, the boat was in the middle of the lake, and He was alone on land. He saw the disciples straining at the oars, because the wind was against them. About the fourth watch of the night He went out to them, walking on the lake.

JESUS HAD JUST prayed in public. He gave thanks to His Father for the seemingly insufficient food of five loaves and two fish for over 5,000 people. He demonstrated that prayer is an exercise in faith, an exercise of trust in a God who can do more than we ask.

The crowd was satisfied and was now strengthened for their journey back to their homes. Certainly they had witnessed the power of prayer. Prayer really works! Jesus sent them away with the knowledge that God cares for both their spiritual and physical needs.

But Jesus was not satisfied with just praying in public. He would demonstrate how much He valued praying and communing privately with His Father. He sent His disciples ahead in a boat and retreated to a lonely place to be alone with His Father. Jesus chose a mountainside, a place where He would not be disturbed or be hurried.

It was evening, before dark, when He began His private prayer time with His Father. This, according to Roman reckoning of time, was the first watch of the night. The night was divided into four watches, the first called the "evening" watch, the second "midnight," the third "cockcrow," and the fourth the "morning" watch. Jesus, therefore, spent all night, from the evening watch until the fourth watch, in prayer, praying from evening till morning. After this all-night prayer time with His Father, Jesus rejoined His disciples on the lake, just at daybreak.

As Jesus here demonstrated, prayer is peaceful communion and fellowship with God, unhurried time in God's presence. What Jesus said during this night of prayer seems not to be what's important, for it is not revealed. The lesson for us is that He spent all night alone with His Father. We too need and should seek private and unhurried time with our heavenly Father.

Prayer, then, is our heart reaching out to God's heart, our minds reaching out to God's infinite mind. Prayer is humble submission of one's self in the presence of a holy God.

After such an awesome experience all night in fellowship and communion with His Father, Jesus came to His disciples, walking on the water at daybreak. What a contrast: the disciples struggled all night on the lake, trying to reach the shore, but Jesus was at peace because of the time He spent in prayer with His Father during the night. It is no wonder that His life displayed so much power and might! His powerful life was the result of the private, unhurried time spent with His Father.

Questions for Reflection

1) Why did Jesus retreat to a mountainside to pray?

2) What was Jesus demonstrating by praying all night to His Father?

3) For what should we seek most when we pray?

Prayer

Thank You, Lord Jesus, for showing me the importance of fellowship and communion with God our Father. Teach me to spend time, unhurried time, in His holy presence. Grant me the desire to pray as You did, to experience the peace that comes in answer to prayer. May this be my joyful privilege. This I pray, in Your mighty name. Amen.

Lesson 7

PRAYER AND SUBMISSION TO GOD'S WILL

Matthew 26:36-39,42

Then Jesus went with His disciples to a place called
Gethsemane, and He said to them, "Sit here while I go over
there and pray." He took Peter and the two sons of Zebedee
along with Him, and He began to be sorrowful and troubled.
38 *Then He said to them, "My soul is overwhelmed with sorrow*
to the point of death. Stay here and keep watch with me." Going
a little farther, He fell with His face to the ground and prayed,
"My Father, if it is possible, may this cup be taken from me.
Yet not as I will, but as you will. . . ." He went away a second
time and prayed, "My Father, if it is not possible for this cup
to be taken away unless I drink it, may Your will be done."

JESUS, THE VERY night He was betrayed and arrested, prepared for this ordeal with prayer. First we must note that yesterday's prayer is insufficient for today's problems. Each day we need a fresh supply of God's grace to meet the new challenges for that day. Although Jesus prayed every day, He would not depend on past blessings to cope with present challenges, so He prayed again on that fateful night of His arrest.

Next we discover that prayer is personal. While it is good for others to pray for you, it is no substitute for your personal communion with God. Jesus invited His disciples to join Him in prayer, but He prayed for Himself as well, a little distance from them.

Third, prayer is submission to the will of our heavenly Father. Jesus prayed, "Yet not as I will, but as You will" and "May Your will be done." Prayer is giving control of ourselves over to God. It is recognizing that our heavenly Father is ruler of heaven and earth, and our desires are to be subject to His control.

To pray in faith is to accept that God may not always grant us relief, but He will give us of His grace to endure whatever He allows. Prayer in faith is accepting that God knows best, and that we can trust Him, especially in times of danger.

Prayer, therefore, is not an escape from the realities of life or the dangers that confront us, but the firm trust that "even though I walk through the valley of the shadow of death, I will fear no evil," for my Father in heaven is with me and He will comfort me (Psalm 23:3,4).

Believing prayer is accepting that, in all things, God works for the good of those who love and trust Him, and that He has a divine purpose for each of us (Romans 8:28).

Questions for Reflection

1) Jesus prayed daily. Why then was it necessary for Him to pray just before His arrest in Gethsemane?

2) Prayer does not remove all problems and difficulties from our lives, why then should we pray?

3) What does it mean to submit to the will of God?

Prayer

Dear Lord, I recognize I need You at all times to be in control of my life. Teach me to trust You and let Your will be done, for You know what is best for me. Thank You for the assurance that Your grace will sustain me through each day and comfort me with heaven's peace. Amen.

PRAYER AND YOUR WILL

LUKE 22:39-46

Jesus went out as usual to the Mount of Olives, and His disciples followed Him. On reaching the place, He said to them, "Pray that you will not fall into temptation." He withdrew about a stone's throw beyond them, knelt down and prayed, "Father, if Your are willing, take this cup from me; yet not my will, but Yours be done." An angel from heaven appeared to Him and strengthened Him. And being in anguish, He prayed more earnestly, and His sweat was like drops of blood falling to the ground.

When He rose from prayer and went back to the disciples, [H]e found them asleep, exhausted from sorrow.
46 "Why are you sleeping?" He asked them. "Get up and pray so that you will not fall into temptation."

JESUS KNEW THAT His arrest and crucifixion were imminent. Because daily communion with His father was His practice, His natural response was to seek His Father's counsel as danger approached. Our Lord retreated to His accustomed praying place, Mount Olivet, His prayer garden. This was His prayer closet.

Jesus knew that the only path to victory over temptation was prayer, so He instructed His disciples to "pray that you will not fall into temptation." Daily we are confronted by temptations, large and small. Prayer, which is communion and fellowship with our Father in heaven, is the only avenue available to us for making right decisions when tempted.

Our Savior was now confronting His greatest temptation. Should He go to the cross to save the world or should He retreat to the safety of heaven? Should He die for mankind or should He save His own life? What choice should He make? What choice would His father have Him make?

This experience of Jesus teaches us that prayer is the surrender of the "will," which is "the power of choice." Our will is our freedom to choose. To overcome temptation, our will, or freedom to choose, must be surrendered to God. We must ask our heavenly Father to guide us in our decision-making, large or small, and only when we are in daily communion with Him are we able to discern His voice.

When the will is surrendered, God gives us strength to face our temptations. Prayer does not always remove us from evil or danger but gives us courage and strength to face it. Prayer may not always rescue us from suffering, but heaven's strength, heaven's grace is given to uphold us. For Jesus, "an angel from heaven appeared to Him and strengthened Him" (Luke 23:43).

The surrender of the will is not an easy task. It is the total abandonment of self, and a humble, childlike trust in God. For Jesus, this surrender was so difficult that it produced physical symptoms: sweat—bloody-looking sweat. Surrender is a fierce battle of the will. Should I decide or should I let God decide and I humbly obey? Giving back our freedom to make decisions to God is a constant struggle, a daily struggle, and only through earnest and constant prayer can this be accomplished.

The reason our world is in such a sad and sinful state is because most of us make our own decisions. God's will is not done—ours is done. No wonder Jesus taught us to pray, "Thy will be done on earth as it is in heaven" (Matthew 6:10)!

Salvation is free, but to accept it costs us everything. Salvation is the total surrender to the Lordship of Christ, the giving up of our freedom to choose, back to the control of God who gave it. Only then are we truly free, for if God does not guide our choosing, the Devil will, and he does not seek our permission.

Questions for Reflection

1) What was Jesus driven to do as the danger of His arrest and crucifixion approached?

2) How can prayer for communion with God affect or choices and decisions?

3) How does prayer relate to the surrender of the will?

Prayer

Dear Lord, I praise You for Jesus my Savior who surrendered His will to Your control and died to save me. Teach me also to surrender my will, to surrender myself to Your control. Save me from evil temptations. Give me grace to trust You, and may my life give glory to You. Amen.

PRAYER AND VICTORY OVER TEMPTATION

MATTHEW 26:40,41

Then He returned to His disciples and found them sleeping. "Could you men not keep watch with Me for one hour?" He asked Peter. "Watch and pray so that you will not fall into temptation. The spirit is willing, but the body is weak."

JESUS, WHILE ENDURING severe agony as He struggled over our sins, gave this sober warning to His sleeping friends: "Watch and pray that you will not fall into temptation...."

He wanted His disciples to know that communion and fellowship with God is the only buffer against temptation. We cannot overcome temptation in our own strength.

All sin results from not being in constant communion and fellowship with Jesus and His father. Prayer focuses the mind on Jesus, who has already won the victory over sin for us. Prayer places our trust not in our own ability, but in God who alone can give us victory.

Prayer that brings victory is not a hurried exercise. Jesus asked His sleeping disciples, "Could you not watch with Me one hour?" Jesus was praying for an hour, at least, and He is our example in prayer. Three times He went off alone to pray, so He spent more than one hour in communion with His Father. As we have seen, communion and fellowship that gives victory to our lives requires time, unhurried time with our Lord.

Making time for prayer requires the force of the will. Our lives are full of activity; we are always busy, always doing something. However, prayer is so essential each day that we must choose to make it a priority. Finding time to pray is not easy—in fact, it is not as natural to pray as we think. It is one of the most difficult battles in life, to find unhurried time to pray. We can become so tired as we go through our many activities each day, working, traveling, caring for children, etc., that we are drained doing good things.

That's why Jesus warned that "the spirit is willing but the flesh is weak." We may want to pray, but our tired bodies prevent us. It is therefore best to begin the day with unhurried prayer, an hour with the Lord of our lives. Can we not devote one of the twenty-four hours of each day to communion and fellowship with our Father who loves and cares for us?

Questions for Reflection

1) Can we overcome temptation through our own strength and will?

2) What causes us to sin?

3) How important is it to slow down and take time for unhurried prayer?

Prayer

Holy Father, I seek You, for You are my defense in times of temptation. Remind me daily to slow down and seek Your companionship so that I can live a victorious life. Grant me the desire to trust Your leading in my life, that I may live for Your glory. Amen.

Lesson 10

PRAYER— GOD'S SURVIVAL TOOL

Luke 21:34-36

"Be careful, or your hearts will be weighed down with carousing, drunkenness and the anxieties of life, and that day will close on you suddenly like a trap. For it will come on all those who live on the face of the whole earth. Be always on the watch, and pray that you may be able to escape all that is about to happen, and that you may be able to stand before the Son of Man."

JESUS, JUST BEFORE He made this statement, painted a tragic picture of the world as it hurries to its inevitable climax. This world will come to an end. Sin has doomed this world to destruction.

Jesus, however, shows the loving heart of God through His revelation of the events that will engulf our world. He tells us how we can be prepared so that we can know the meaning of these events and live with hope. Prayer is God's survival tool for living through these terrible events.

These tragic events are occurring today. Nations at war, revolutions, natural disasters, these are all signs of the end. Persecution for believing in Jesus and the breakdown of family relationships are also signs that the world is hastening to its close. Fear and anxiety will grip many as they experience these frightening and tragic events.

There can be no doubt that a general fear is overtaking the nation. Parents are fearful for their children. They can be gunned down at or on their way to and from school. Anxiety is heightened even more when, for the sake of profit and the false belief that each individual must defend himself, more guns are purchased, making the society less safe. The recent tragedy in South Africa, the blade runner Oscar Pistorius, who captivated the world during the London Olympics, shot and killed his fiancée in his home, thinking she was a burglar. This highlights the fallacy that guns make us safer. Guns can only increase fear and make us more vulnerable to an untimely death. Did Jesus not give the warning that those who live by the sword will die by the sword? (Matthew 26:52)

Jesus, therefore, gives us the true remedy, the only tool that can keep us secure in this anxious and dangerous world. The tool, of course, is prayer, reliance on God who alone can keep us safe. Prayer is the only sure cure for a life of anxiety and fear.

Prayer also keeps us watchful, as these tragic and destructive events that are signs of the end continue to occur. It keeps our focus on the return of our Savior, who promised He will come again. Instead of living anxious lives, we can live lives of hope. We can live with expectancy, for prayer will always remind us that our rescue, our final redemption, is near.

Only those who pray, those who daily commune with heaven will be prepared for the coming of Jesus. Only they will be able to stand, to rejoice, for through prayer they will have come to know Jesus their Savior and His Father who sent Him to save us.

Questions for Reflection

1) To what do the tragic events in our world point?

2) What is the tool God gave for our survival in these days and how should it be used?

3) How does prayer prepare us for the soon return of Jesus?

Prayer

Loving Lord, I thank You for revealing to me Your tool for my survival in an evil and tragedy-filled world. I rejoice, for I can come to You daily and trust You for my protection, and receive hope as I await Your return when sin and evil will be ended. Come, Lord Jesus, come quickly. I long for that glorious day of victory, that day of joy when I will see You and our Father face-to-face. Come, I pray, O Lord, come. Amen.

Lesson 11

Praying Through the Night

Luke 6:12

One of those days Jesus went out to a mountainside to pray, and spent the night praying to God.

Jesus had power to perform miracles. Luke records that He healed a paralyzed man who was lowered through the roof of the house. He also healed a man's right hand that was deformed. Jesus also forgave sin. His was a powerful life.

It is therefore very instructive to us that Jesus did not rely on the power He had to perform miracles for His daily living. He sought private time to be with His Father to receive new strength and wisdom. He was preparing to choose twelve close followers, and He sought His Father's direction. He "spent the night praying to God."

There are important lessons we can learn from this act

of Jesus. First, we should not be satisfied with yesterday's blessings but seek daily a fresh supply of God's grace. We need renewed power to live each day, and we therefore must seek it each day.

Second, prayer is unhurried time in companionship and a fellowship with God. It is entering into God's presence. To pray is to recognize that you are seeking audience with a holy God, your heavenly Father, and that's a very high privilege. When you experience this awesome privilege, you want it to last. You are in no haste to end it. Your desire to be in your Father's presence grows. Jesus experienced this unique privilege powerfully, so He spent all night praying.

Third, when one spends unhurried time with God, he or she can listen for His voice. In the stillness and quietness of that sacred time, our minds can become alert to impressions from heaven. It is during these sacred moments that the will of God is more clearly discerned. Better choices and decisions are made. The clutter of life's cares and anxieties are swept away, and the assurance of God's leading brings peace. Doubt and fear are replaced by confidence and conviction as the mind becomes renewed in God's presence.

It is our privilege to fellowship with our heavenly Father each day for renewed strength and wisdom to make wise choices, as Jesus did.

Questions for Reflection

1) Jesus lived a powerful life. Why did He need to pray so often?

2) Why is it a good practice to pray daily?

3) What benefits can be received through unhurried times in prayer?

Prayer

O Lord, help me to realize that spending time with You is a blessed privilege. Forgive me for not appreciating how precious the time spent with You in prayer is. Give me the desire to experience Your love and friendship. May I hear Your voice and discern the way You are leading in my life. This I pray, in the name of Jesus my Savior. Amen.

Lesson 12

THE TRANSFORMING POWER OF PRAYER

Luke 9:28-36

About eight days after Jesus said this, He took Peter, John and James with Him and went up onto a mountain to pray. As He was praying, the appearance of His face changed, and His clothes became as bright as a flash of lightning. Two men, Moses and Elijah, appeared in glorious splendor, talking with Jesus. They spoke about His departure, which He was about to bring to fulfillment at Jerusalem. Peter and his companions were very sleepy, but when they became fully awake, they saw His glory and the two men standing with Him. As the men were leaving Jesus, Peter said to Him, "Master, it is good for us to be here. Let us put up three shelters—one for you, one for Moses and one for Elijah." (He did not know what he was saying.) While he was speaking, a cloud appeared and enveloped them, and they were afraid as they entered the cloud. A voice came from the cloud, saying, "This is my Son, whom I have chosen; listen to Him." When the voice had spoken, they found that Jesus was alone. The disciples kept this to themselves, and told no one at that time what they had seen.

JESUS OFTEN PRAYED in private. He loved being alone with His Father. However, on significant occasions, He invited others to join Him in prayer.

On this occasion He invited his closest friends, Peter, James, and John, and again Jesus spent hours in prayer, for His companions became sleepy. It would seem that Jesus wanted to teach His close disciples the nature and power of prayer.

As Jesus prayed, His appearance changed as the glory of His Father descended upon Him. His face lighted up, even His clothes shone like bright lights. Heaven came down to earth for a brief period as a result of prayer and communion with God.

We also, when we truly pray and commune with our heavenly Father, can have a like experience. Moses, a man just like us, had a similar experience after being with God for forty days. His face shone and the Israelites became afraid, so he veiled his face while he talked with them. This is how the experience of Moses is described:

> *When Moses came down from Mount Sinai with the two tablets of the Testimony in his hands, he was not aware that his face was radiant because he had spoken with the LORD. When Aaron and all the Israelites saw Moses, his face was radiant, and they*

> *were afraid to come near him. But Moses called to them; so Aaron and all the leaders of the community came back to him, and he spoke to them. Afterward all the Israelites came near him, and he gave them all the commands the* Lord *had given him on Mount Sinai. When Moses finished speaking to them, he put a veil over his face. But whenever he entered the* Lord*'s presence to speak with him, he removed the veil until he came out. And when he came out and told the Israelites what he had been commanded, they saw that his face was radiant. Then Moses would put the veil back over his face until he went in to speak with the* Lord*.* (Exodus 34:29-35)

Prayer is certainly entering into the presence of a holy God. What a privilege!

Heaven's help also comes in answer to prayer. Jesus received support, strength, and encouragement to face His crucifixion. Moses, whose face also lighted up when in the presence of God, came to be with Jesus at the Transfiguration, proving that the death of Jesus guarantees our resurrection. Elijah, who did not die but was taken up to heaven, also came to prove that the sacrifice of Jesus also guarantees that when the Savior returns, many will be taken to heaven without experiencing death. That was the help Jesus needed. We too can and will receive the help we need when we sincerely pray to our Father in heaven.

The voice of God can be heard when we pray. It may

not be audible as it was for the three friends of Jesus, but God will speak to our minds. His voice of acceptance will be heard, giving us assurance and guidance. We can never be the same after we have truly communed with God. Our entire lives will be changed, and even our outward appearance will be transformed. Could it be that Jesus wanted His disciples, and us, to know that when we daily commune with Him and His father, Their glory will be displayed and seen through us? Then we will become the light of the world as Jesus said we should be. God's glory will shine through us, in our homes, in our communities, and wherever we are.

Questions for Reflection

1) What may be the reason Jesus invited His close disciples to accompany Him up the mountain to pray?

2) What blessings can we expect when we experience the privilege of prayer?

3) How may we become the light of the world as Jesus said we should be?

Prayer

Heavenly Father, thank You for the example of Jesus that reveals how heaven responds when we pray sincerely. May we, through prayer, experience the joy that comes from Your assurance that we are Your children. We praise You for the privilege of reflecting Your glory. Make us eager for this joyful experience daily, that we can be a blessing to the world. To You we give all the glory and all the praise. Amen.

Lesson 13

NINE THINGS JESUS TAUGHT ABOUT PRAYER

Luke 11:1-13

One day Jesus was praying in a certain place. When He finished, one of His disciples said to Him, "Lord, teach us to pray, just as John taught his disciples."

He said to them, "When you pray, say:

'Father,
hallowed be Your name,
Your kingdom come.
3 Give us each day our daily bread.
4 Forgive us our sins,
for we also forgive everyone who sins against us.

And lead us not into temptation.'"

Then He said to them, "Suppose one of you has a friend, and he goes to him at midnight and says, 'Friend, lend me three loaves of bread, because a friend of mine on a journey has come to me, and I have nothing to set before him.'

"Then the one inside answers, 'Don't bother me. The door is already locked, and my children are with me in bed. I can't get up and give you anything.' I tell you, though he will not get up and give him the bread because he is his friend, yet because of the man's boldness he will get up and give him as much as he needs.

"So I say to you: Ask and it will be given to you; seek and you will find; knock and the door will be opened to you. For everyone who asks receives; he who seeks finds; and to him who knocks, the door will be opened. Which of you fathers, if your son asks for a fish, will give him a snake instead? Or if he asks for an egg, will give him a scorpion? 13 *If you then, though you are evil, know how to give good gifts to your children, how much more will your Father in heaven give the Holy Spirit to those who ask Him!"*

JESUS HAD A regular, daily prayer habit, often holding private conversations with His Father. His disciples were impressed. One day as He ended His prayer time with His Father, one of His disciples made a request: "Lord, teach us to pray, just as John the Baptist taught his followers to pray." Jesus was pleased to answer this request, and gave what may seem a very long answer, in which we find another version of the Lord's Prayer. However, in His response we find a nine point plan for effective prayer. It has been my experience that following this plan will revolutionize your life.

1) **Prayer should be simple.** God is not impressed by many words. There are no magic words to be constantly repeated or chanted. Be simple and be sincere.

2) **Recognize God's holiness in contrast to your sinfulness.** Prayer is seeking audience with a holy God: "Hallowed is His name." God is to be respected and reverenced.

3) **God is in control.** We can be assured that His soon-coming kingdom will be established to replace this sinful world. It is our privilege to pray for this reality, and not be discouraged as we see evil around us. Evil and sin will come to an end.

4) **Pray with confidence for your daily needs.** God does provide. We may not get all we want, but we will receive what we need. Our daily food and needs are His concern.

5) **Forgiveness is received through prayer.** We pray to a forgiving God. His forgiveness enables us, in turn, to forgive others. When one rejoices in heaven's forgiveness, his heart can hold no malice nor seek revenge.

6) **Prayer gives protection.** It keeps us away from the devil's traps to lead us away from God. Temptations are blunted, and they lose their power when we seek our God in prayer. God guides those who sincerely pray.

7) **You can be bold when you pray.** Pray with confidence—do not doubt, and do not be hesitant. Be like the man who boldly and confidently awakes his friend at midnight, seeking what he needed.

8) **Be persistent when you pray.** "Ask," "seek," "knock": Jesus used these words to indicate that prayer is not casual, meaningless talk. It is sincere, earnest seeking after God and His way. God will answer—He will open the door of His grace and blessing to you.

9) **The best gift God can give to us is the Holy Spirit.** He is the one true guide for our lives in this sinful world, and He comes in answer to prayer. God is eager to give Him to us. What a privilege: God the Holy Spirit with us each day!

Prayer as Jesus taught is revolutionary. Why should we ever choose to live a day without this connection with heaven? It is our privilege, joy, and blessing to pray.

Questions for Reflection

1) What effect should the holiness of God have on us when we pray?

2) What example did Jesus use to teach us that we should be earnest and sincere when we pray?

3) What special gift can we receive from God when we ask in prayer?

Prayer

Dear Lord, You are holy, and it is my joy to enter Your presence through prayer. I pray that Your will be done in my life as Your will is done in heaven. Give to me the Holy Spirit, Your promised gift. Keep me safe from the devil's attempts to control my life. Let me never doubt Your willingness to fill my life with Your blessings. Thank You for Your invitation to come to You with confidence, knowing that Your love and grace will sustain me each day. Amen.

Lesson 14

THE NEED FOR PERSISTENCE IN PRAYER

Luke 18:1-8

Then Jesus told His disciples a parable to show them that they should always pray and not give up. He said: "In a certain town there was a judge who neither feared God nor cared about men. And there was a widow in that town who kept coming to him with the plea, 'Grant me justice against my adversary.' For some time he refused. But finally he said to himself, 'Even though I don't fear God or care about men, yet because this widow keeps bothering me, I will see that she gets justice, so that she won't eventually wear me out with her coming!'"

And the Lord said, "Listen to what the unjust judge says. And will not God bring about justice for His chosen ones, who cry out to Him day and night? Will He keep putting them off? I tell you, He will see that they get justice, and quickly. However, when the Son of Man comes, will He find faith on the earth?"

THE DESIRE FOR justice and that it be timely is legitimate. No one feels comfortable when confronted with injustice. It is natural to seek justice and to want it quickly. This story Jesus told reminds us that we live in an unfair world, one in which the weak are at the mercy of the powerful.

Jesus taught that God is a God of justice, and though we live in an unfair society, we can appeal to a just God and He will respond quickly. He will be our defense. Do not lose hope, for God knows that "justice delayed is justice denied."

The Lord ended this parable with the question: "However, when the Son of Man comes, will He find faith on the earth?" Why this question?

Jesus was making the point that our faith is constantly threatened. Injustice or delay of justice can destroy faith in both God and man. There is constant temptation to stop trusting God because He seems unable to protect us. When we pray, the answer seems to be no, or at best, wait. And we wonder, does God hear our prayer? Does prayer work?

But Jesus taught that we should keep on praying. Keep trusting, as a professor in the seminary I attended told the class one day; "Hope is hope when there is no reason to hope." To paraphrase, we should keep on praying when there seems to be no reason to keep on praying.

Persistent prayer shields us from being faithless in an unjust world. Sometimes, it may seem that God is slow to act, and we become impatient, but Jesus teaches that this is the time to persist in prayer. Prayer, persistent prayer, is our defense against the temptation to stop relying on God. Day and night we can and should call to our Father in heaven, the just Judge of all the earth, "that His will be done on earth as it is done in heaven." And because we are God's chosen ones, who trust Him and cry out to Him in prayer, Jesus says our heavenly Father will come to our defense, and do so quickly.

The lesson Jesus taught was that our faith is dependent on our prayers. Genuine, sincere prayer strengthens faith. Prayer reminds us that God who is just and faithful will reward our faith. True faith shines when tested. Trials perfect our faith and cause those who love God to depend on Him even more. Yes, when Jesus comes back to the earth, there will be faith, the faith of those who persist in prayer.

Because we are precious to God, "His chosen ones," we should keep on praying, trusting in a God who cares for His own. We must never give up, never give in, for God, the righteous Judge, is actively working for our good.

Questions for Reflection

1) How does prayer help us retain our faith in the justice of God while we live in an unjust world?

2) Why did Jesus tell this story to His disciples?

3) What did Jesus teach in this lesson on prayer about our status, and relationship to God?

Prayer

Lord of heaven and earth, my Father, I praise You, for You are a God of justice. Thank You that I am Your chosen child, and I can rely on Your love in this unfair world. Help me to humbly come to You each day and trust You for my defense. May I never lose faith in You, the righteous Judge of all the earth. Amen.

Lesson 15

ONLY THE HUMBLE TRULY PRAY

Luke 18:9-14

To some who were confident of their own righteousness and looked down on everybody else, Jesus told this parable: "Two men went up to the temple to pray, one a Pharisee and the other a tax collector. The Pharisee stood up and prayed about himself: 'God, I thank you that I am not like other men—robbers, evildoers, adulterers—or even like this tax collector. I fast twice a week and give a tenth of all I get.'

"But the tax collector stood at a distance. He would not even look up to heaven, but beat his breast and said, 'God, have mercy on me, a sinner.'

"I tell you that this man, rather than the other, went home justified before God. For everyone who exalts himself will be humbled, and he who humbles himself will be exalted."

WHEN WE PRAY we are privileged to enter into communion with a holy and righteous God. This creates in us a humble spirit, a realization that we are sinners. We are never worthy to come before God in prayer, but God accepts and listens to our prayers when we humbly trust in the grace of our Savior, Jesus Christ.

We have all sinned, and our lives do not reflect the glory of a holy God. None of us are righteous; therefore, our cry in prayer should be like that of King David, "Create in me a pure heart, O God, and renew a steadfast spirit within me. Do not cast me from Your presence or take Your Holy Spirit from me" (Psalm 51:12, 13).

We have no righteousness to present before God when we pray. Prayer is not a boast about how good we are, or a recitation of what we think of ourselves, but a cry to God to reveal to us our true selves. True prayer is not about us, but it is about a holy God who welcomes us into His presence and is willing to commune and fellowship with us.

Prayer is not an occasion to compare ourselves with others or think we are better than others. The Scriptures declare, "Pride goes before destruction, a haughty spirit before a fall" (1 Corinthians 10:12). Prayer is a call to humility before God and man.

At best, when we pray, we can only lament our unworthiness and cry out for mercy but rejoice that our righteous and holy Father in heaven accepts us because Jesus paid the price for sins on the cross. Because of Jesus, we can come before God with confidence, knowing He will receive us and give us His peace.

Humility when we pray makes us ready to receive God's cleansing, which lifts us up. Our most elevated position in life, our most exalted stance is to be at peace with God, reconciled to Him, experiencing a saved relationship with our Maker—for everyone who prays with humility is justified (made right with God). We can rise from our prayer knowing that all our sins are forgiven, and we can live lives that are a blessing to others. What a privilege!

Questions for Reflection

1) What disposition should we have when we pray?

2) What is the difference between being "self-righteous" and being blessed with the righteousness of Jesus?

3) Instead of trying to impress God about how good we are, what should we seek when we pray?

Prayer

Lord, I am a sinner. I need Your forgiveness and grace. Reveal to me my true self and change me into Your likeness. Grant me Your righteousness in exchange for my unworthiness. For these blessings, I humbly pray, in the name of Jesus who died for my sins. Amen.

Lesson 16

Prayer and Our Children

Matthew 19:13

Then people brought little children to Jesus for Him to place His hands on them and pray for them. But the disciples rebuked them.

The ministry of Jesus was primarily focused on adults. He was busy teaching, healing, and revealing His Father's love to the grown-ups. They needed a new understanding of God because their traditions and teachings had misrepresented Him.

Impressed with His teachings and seeing how powerful the life of Jesus was, parents brought their children to Him for blessings and prayer. These parents must have noticed the powerful effects of the prayers of Jesus.

The disciples, however, thought that praying and receiving blessings were for adults only. Praying for children was an unnecessary burden that should not slow the work of Jesus. But Jesus corrected the false view His disciples had by calling the little children and revealing that they too need the blessings that come through prayer. Jesus was demonstrating that our children should be exposed to prayer and learn of its benefits.

Now that Jesus is no longer physically present on earth, parents can still bring their children to Him for His blessing through prayer. Our children, as they grow, should be taught that they too can speak with the God of the universe. They should know Him as a friend and feel happy in His presence. Parents are to be examples in prayer before their children. Let them observe Mom and Dad spending unhurried time with Jesus, and by observing, they will learn that time spent with God is precious. Parents can create a heavenly atmosphere in the home that can be a blessing to their children for all their lives. Parents should help their children to appreciate time with Jesus above television, electronic games and sports. How novel that would be!

What a difference the lives of our children and our communities would be if more of our children were taught to pray! They would learn that they are children of our heavenly Father and that they are precious to Him. They would learn to be kind and loving to others. Teaching our children to pray at an early age can protect them from destructive behaviors that are ever present in our society!

Children are more honest, sincere, and transparent than most adults. Their prayers are most precious to Jesus, for they have no pretense. No wonder Jesus said, "Let the little children come to me, and do not hinder them, for the kingdom of heaven belongs to such as these."

Questions for Reflection

1) Why do you think parents brought their children to Jesus?

2) How can children learn the value of prayer from the parents?

3) Why did Jesus say about children, "The kingdom of heaven belongs to such as these?"

Prayer

Loving Jesus, thank You for revealing that all children are precious to You and our heavenly Father. Teach us parents that it is our privilege and duty to present our children to You and to seek Your blessing on their lives. May our children, who are gifts from You, come to know You and love You. As they grow, make them blessings to others. This we pray in Your holy name. Amen.

PRAYER AND WATCHFULNESS

LUKE 21:34-36

"Be careful, or your hearts will be weighed down with dissipation, drunkenness and the anxieties of life, and that day will close on you unexpectedly like a trap. For it will come upon all those who live on the face of the whole earth. Be always on the watch, and pray that you may be able to escape all that is about to happen, and that you may be able to stand before the Son of Man."

THIS PASSAGE THAT was referenced in Lesson 10 reveals more than was discussed, so let us take a second look at it.

This world will come to an end, and as it hastens on to its inevitable climax, we must be alert. We need to be careful about how we live.

Living in an evil and sinful world affects us all. We are

entertained by violence and immorality. Love and respect for others is in decline. The effects of an evil world are clearly seen in the lives of those who do not know God. Those who do not know God do not seek communion and fellowship with Him through prayer. Some live lives full of worry, anxiety and fear. Others live for the present, unconscious or unconcerned about their future destiny.

A life of prayer, in contrast, results in the consciousness that God is in control and that He will bring evil to an end at the coming of Jesus. Many will be unprepared and surprised when Jesus comes again because they were not watchful through prayer. The person who does not live a life of prayer will live a careless life, a life without self-control, a life of indulgence, an immoral life, a life without restraint. The person who does not pray lacks the inner strength to overcome the evils present in our world.

Some may suggest that one does not need to believe in God to live a good life. There are many who live morally and do much good that bless the lives of others. But the warning of Jesus still applies, for all must stand before Him when He returns. No matter how good a person's life may be, without a connection to Jesus, he is in danger. The Savior's call to be watchful and pray is relevant for all. The return of Jesus is an event that will affect all, believer and non-believer, religious and non-religious, but only those who are always watching and always praying will be ready for that climactic event.

Life presents only two options: accept Jesus and live as He says we should, and be blessed with the reward He promised, or reject Him, believing He is irrelevant, and accept the consequences of our choice. For those who choose Jesus, His word is, be always watchful by always praying.

The one who prays and enjoys fellowship and communion with God is protected from the evils that have engulfed our world. He will be kept in peace and live with expectant hope that he will be soon rescued from this world of sin when Jesus our Lord and Savior returns. Prayer inoculates and protects us against living a wasteful and meaningless life, a life without hope. A prayerful life is one of joyful hope and eager expectation of our final liberation from a sin cursed world, the day when, like Dr. King, we will shout, "Free at last, free at last, thank God Almighty we are free at last!"

Questions for Reflection

1) Of what does prayer remind us as we live in this sinful world?

2) Prayer protects us from living what kind of life?

3) From what are we protected when we commune with God in prayer?

Prayer

Gracious Father, thank You for the privilege of prayer. Thank You for the protection from evil that I receive in answer to my prayer. Keep me ever alert and expectant as I await the return of my Savior who will bring evil to an end. I trust in Your grace that will enable me to stand before Jesus when He returns. In His name, I pray. Amen.

PRAY—GOD IS LISTENING

John 11:41,42

So they took away the stone. Then Jesus looked up and said, "Father, I thank You that You have heard me. I knew that You always hear me, but I said this for the benefit of the people standing here, that they may believe that You sent Me."

Lazarus, a close friend and follower of Jesus, was dead and buried for four days. His sisters, Martha and Mary, had sent for Jesus, confident that He could restore their brother's health.

Jesus, however, did not respond as they expected. He allowed Lazarus to die, then traveled to Bethany and arrived, so it seemed, four days late.

There was no doubt that Jesus had the power to heal Lazarus and restore his health. He had, just days before, healed a man born blind. Why did He not respond quickly to His friend's urgent need and cure him of his illness? Jesus knew Lazarus would die; in fact, He knew exactly when he died. He deliberately allowed Lazarus to die because He wanted His followers to learn significant lessons about prayer and His dependence on His Father.

What lessons were so significant that He allowed His close friend to die and cause such pain and disappointment for Mary and Martha, whom He also loved? Jesus Himself wept because of their pain and sadness. However, His prayer reveals a comforting truth that we need, for it gives us confidence when we pray.

"Father," Jesus prayed, "I thank You that You have heard me. I knew that You always hear Me, but I said this for the benefit of the people standing here, that they may believe that You sent Me."

Jesus wants us to know who He is. Prayer is the recognition of who Jesus is, the One sent by the Father to save us from sin. Prayer focuses the mind on Christ and His amazing sacrifice to redeem us. Prayer is a call to our loving Father who gave His best, His one and only Son to die in our place.

Jesus, as He prayed, was also revealing that just as Lazarus died and would soon be raised from the dead, so too would He, our Savior, die and be raised to guarantee our salvation.

The Father whom Jesus prayed to is a God who listens. Jesus wanted His followers to know this important truth. Our Father in heaven listens to every sincere prayer. God is mindful of our needs, so we can pray with assurance.

Nothing that concerns us is unimportant to our heavenly Father.

The Savior also revealed that true prayer should be full of thanksgiving. Even in the worst of circumstances, we should give thanks. God always listens to us when we pray, and for that, we should be thankful.

Jesus thanked His Father before He received the answer to His prayer. We too, when we pray, should always give thanks to our heavenly Father as we await His blessings. Prayer is a call to faith, a call to trust, a call to believe. We pray because we expect God to act, and we should thank Him in advance for what He will do. True prayer is much more than making requests—it is praise and thanksgiving.

Questions for Reflection

1) Of what does prayer remind us about Jesus?

2) Of what does the prayer of Jesus at Lazarus' tomb remind us?

3) What can we learn from Jesus' giving thanks to His Father before raising Lazarus to life?

Prayer

Holy Father, it is a blessing to know that You always listen to my prayer. Increase my faith. Teach me to trust You more and more and to be always thankful, no matter the circumstances, for You are a God who answers sincere prayer. To You be all praise, honor and glory, for You are a gracious and generous God. Amen.

LESSON 19

PRAYER—THE SECRET OF A POWERFUL LIFE

LUKE 5:16

But Jesus often withdrew to lonely places and prayed.

JESUS HAD JUST healed a man with the dreaded disease of leprosy. How interesting that Jesus told the healed a man "Don't tell anyone," but news of this great miracle spread and crowds came to be healed and to hear His message of hope. Luke clues us in on the habit, the custom of Jesus: that He would often get away from the crowd and spend one on one time with his Father.

Christ had power to heal, and He had a message of grace to share. He could have kept on healing and preaching, but Jesus did what may seem, to us, unnecessary. He would "often withdraw to lonely places" and pray. Jesus never allowed Himself to be swept along by His successes so that He felt He could do His Father's work on His own.

It is so easy to be blinded with success that we forget the source of our success. Jesus never forgot. He depended on regular communion and fellowship with His Father. He never forgot He was doing the work of His Father, not His own. To His Father, He gave credit for all His accomplishments. Our Savior demonstrated how to handle success. Run to God in prayer and be humbled that He granted you the privilege to do something for His glory. Whatever we do should not be about us, but it should always point to our gracious God.

Prayer, therefore, protects us from taking to ourselves the credit for the good we do. It reminds us of the source of our strength, the real power that works through us. It is extremely difficult and well-nigh impossible to boast when we are in regular communion with God during the day. Prayer is a constant reminder that we have nothing to boast about before God or man.

Jesus prayed in private because He had nothing to boast about, and He enjoyed fellowship with His Father. It is for our good that we should follow His example. Praying in public can sometimes be an occasion for boasting and self-promotion. Private prayer tempers our public behavior and causes us to give all the glory and praise to God who alone is worthy.

Prayer is a call to retreat from the busyness of life and be alone with God. It is always best to begin each day with prayer, but it is also necessary to pause from the busy activities and refocus our lives on our heavenly Father and our Savior, Jesus Christ.

This Jesus did. We can be tempted to become so involved with work, even working for God, that we forget He is the source of our strength. The example of Jesus was to "often" withdraw to lonely or quiet places to spend time alone with His Father.

If Jesus, who is God, needed time alone with His Father, and would do this often, how much more do we need such fellowship with our Father in heaven? Prayer is therefore a call to live a balanced life. We too should "often" take time out to converse with our heavenly Father. We should never become so busy that regular communion with God becomes a casualty.

Like Jesus, we too should retreat for quiet and private communion with our Father in heaven, especially when we are engaged in His work of saving sinners. Our strength and courage are renewed as we face obstacles and as we face disappointments. We are reminded that it is not by our own might, nor by our own power that we can be successful in doing the work of God. Prayer keeps us humble. Frequent, private communion with heaven keeps us grounded. We remember, as we fellowship with the God of the universe, that we are blessed and privileged to be used by Him in His mission of salvation. All praise and glory belong to the Father, the Son, and the Holy Spirit.

Questions for Reflection

1) To what is prayer a call?

2) From what can prayer protect us?

3) How does private prayer affect our public praying?

Prayer

Lord Jesus, teach me to slow down and come to You, the source of my strength. I repent of my pride and give to You the glory for all my achievements. Let me never forget that to work for You is a privilege, and to You belong all the praise and all the glory. Thanks for choosing and using me in Your service. Help me to realize how much I need You to live a balanced life. May I cherish my daily private moments in Your holy presence and in the presence of our heavenly Father. Amen.

Lesson 20

Prayer and Faith

Mark 11:20-24

In the morning, as they went along, they saw the fig tree withered from the roots. Peter remembered and said to Jesus, "Rabbi, look! The fig tree you cursed has withered!" "Have faith in God," Jesus answered. "I tell you the truth, if anyone says to this mountain, 'Go, throw yourself into the sea,' and does not doubt in his heart but believes that what he says will happen, it will be done for him. Therefore I tell you, whatever you ask for in prayer, believe that you have received it, and it will be yours. And when you stand praying, if you hold anything against anyone, forgive them, so that your Father in heaven may forgive you your sins.

Prayer is much more than words. It is trust, faith, complete confidence in the God to whom we pray.

Jesus used this dramatic example to teach His

disciples the importance of faith when they pray. The purpose of prayer is to build faith in God, to remove doubt, and to grow in trust and confidence that God is able to do for us what we ask.

Prayer is therefore an opportunity to come to God with confidence. Not self-confidence but conviction that the God to whom we pray is the all-powerful God who created this world and holds power over trees and mountains, over all of nature. He can make any tree wither or move any Mountain, if He so desires.

Because prayer is entering into the presence of a holy God and our lives are transformed as we fellowship and commune with Him, our requests, when we pray, should not be selfish. Our requests will be attuned to God's will for us. We can therefore have confidence that our heavenly Father will grant what we ask, for it would be what He desires for us. I doubt anyone would request a fig tree cursed or a mountain moved, but Jesus used these as examples to impress upon us how confident we can be when we pray.

To have this confidence, this strong faith, we must come to know God personally through regular, daily times of prayer, fellowship, and communion. This kind of faith is not built by an occasional prayer when we are in a crisis. We will not have confidence if we pray only when we need something or we find ourselves in a desperate situation of our own making. Daily prayer for communion and fellowship builds our faith and gives us confidence to face any crisis or urgent need. Then whatever we ask for in prayer, it is our privilege to believe and trust our heavenly Father to grant our request.

Jesus placed belief before receiving. He said, "Therefore I tell you, whatever you ask for in prayer, believe that you have received it, and it will be yours." Belief, therefore, is focused on who God is, not necessarily on the answer to our prayer. "Have faith in God," Jesus said. Faith is trusting, depending, and waiting on God. We believe that God will perform, so we wait expectantly for God's answer. Praise and thanks should be given to God even before our prayers are answered.

According to Mark, Jesus included something that may seem strange as He concluded this teaching on prayer and faith. Jesus said, " If you hold anything against anyone, forgive him, so that your Father in heaven may forgive your sins." What does this have to do with faith? To pray with faith, one must have a clean heart. We cannot have evil thoughts on our minds and at the same time pray with faith. We need God's cleansing grace as a prerequisite to prayers that receive answers from God.

Could it be that the greatest answer to prayer that we can ever receive is God's forgiveness that creates in us the willingness to forgive others? Forgiving others can be like a great mountain, but Jesus says it can be thrown into the sea if we have faith in God. The Lord can give us victory over the most difficult and the seemingly insurmountable obstacles in all lives. He says, ask with confidence, do not doubt, and it will be done.

Questions for Reflection

1) How do we develop confidence and strong faith in God?

2) What is the purpose of prayer that Jesus sought to teach His disciples?

3) What prerequisite is necessary for receiving answers to our prayers?

Prayer

Lord, teach me to be sincere when I pray. Give me faith to believe and trust in You. Grant that my requests be according to Your will. May my confidence in You grow stronger each day, as I come before You in prayer. Amen.

Lesson 21

SEVEN LESSONS FROM THIS PRAYER OF JESUS

John 17:1-5

After Jesus said this, He looked toward heaven and prayed:

"Father, the time has come. Glorify your Son, that Your Son may glorify You. For You granted Him authority over all people that He might give eternal life to all those You have given Him. Now this is eternal life: that they may know You, the only true God, and Jesus Christ, whom You have sent. I have brought You glory on earth by completing the work You gave me to do. And now, Father, glorify Me in Your presence with the glory I had with You before the world began."

Jesus often prayed alone and in secret with His Father. On some occasions, however, He prayed in the presence of His disciples, allowing them to be blessed through His prayer. On this occasion, Jesus prayed this amazing prayer from which we can learn seven significant lessons.

1) Prayer is submission to our heavenly Father, submission to His rule over our lives. Jesus prayed, "Father." He begins His prayer with a title of respect, and a name that denotes closeness and that speaks of trust.

2) Prayer recognizes God as the originator and controller of time. "The time has come," Jesus prayed. God acts in time and on time. He knows the right time to act. In the fullness of time, at the right time, Jesus came to earth to redeem us. Now, Jesus acknowledged, the time had come when He must offer Himself on the cross for our sins. This was His Father's time to act, a time set even before the creation of our world. The time for our redemption to be consummated had come, and His Father was in control.

3) Prayer is an act of honoring God, and those who honor God are honored by Him. God first honors us, and the more He does, the more our lives give honor and glory to Him. So Jesus prayed, "Glorify Your son, that Your son may glorify You." We have no praise or honor to offer to God but what He has given us. We can only give what we have received from Him. Praise is always a response to God's goodness.

4) Prayer recognizes our heavenly Father is the giver of eternal life through His Son, Jesus. The Father gave authority to Jesus to give eternal life to all who respond to His love. "For God so loved the world that he gave his

one and only son, that whoever believes in him shall not perish but have eternal life." (John 3:16).

Salvation comes to us by the will of the Father and true prayer is our acceptance of God's will to save us. Jesus submitted to the authority of His Father to grant us eternal life. We, therefore, must also submit to the authority of the Father in accepting eternal life. That's why we pray.

5) Prayer gives us knowledge. What knowledge? The knowledge of eternal life. Jesus prayed, "Now this is eternal life: that they may <u>know</u> you, the only true God, and Jesus whom you have sent." Eternal life is *knowing*, *believing*, and *trusting* our heavenly Father and Jesus His Son.

Prayer opens our minds to a knowledge that makes us trust and have confidence that we are redeemed and reconciled to our heavenly Father through Jesus who gave His life for us.

6) Prayer opens our minds to accept the revelation from the Father that Jesus gave. Jesus said to Thomas, "If you really knew me you would know my father as well..." (John 14:7).

- Jesus revealed that the Father loves us.
- Jesus revealed the Father forgives us.
- Jesus revealed the Father sacrifices for us.
- Jesus revealed the Father endures pain for us.

Jesus completed His mission, the mission to reveal the true nature and heart of His heavenly Father.

7) Prayer is the acceptance of the completed work of Christ who now reigns in the very presence of the Father in heaven. Jesus has reclaimed the glory He had with the Father before this world was created. Jesus is Lord, equal with the Father from eternity past.

Prayer is the high privilege of trusting in God our heavenly Father who ransomed us through Jesus Christ our Lord. Let us embrace it!

Questions for Reflection

1) What can we learn from Jesus beginning His prayer with, "Father"?

2) How can we accept salvation that is offered to us by the will of the Father?

3) What knowledge can we gain through prayer?

Prayer

O God, You are the ruler of time. My time, my life is in Your hands. Teach me to use it wisely. Thank you for being my Father, and may my life give praise to You daily. Grant me eternal life and reveal to me more and more of Your love and grace that sustain me as I await the return of my Lord who reigns with You in heaven. For this I humbly pray, in the Savior's name. Amen.

Lesson 22

PRAYER AND THE MISSION OF JESUS, PART I

John 17:9-19

"I pray for them. I am not praying for the world, but for those You have given Me, for they are Yours. All I have is Yours, and all You have is mine. And glory has come to Me through them. I will remain in the world no longer, but they are still in the world, and I am coming to You. Holy Father, protect them by the power of Your name—the name You gave Me—so that they may be one as We are one. While I was with them, I protected them and kept them safe by that name You gave Me. None has been lost except the one doomed to destruction so that Scripture would be fulfilled.

"I am coming to You now, but I say these things while I am still in the world, so that they may have the full measure of My joy within them. I have given them Your word and the world has hated them, for they are not of the world any more than I am of the world. My prayer is not that You

take them out of the world but that You protect them from the evil one. They are not of the world, even as I am not of it. Sanctify them by the truth; Your word is truth. As You sent Me into the world, I have sent them into the world. For them I sanctify Myself, that they too may be truly sanctified."

JESUS IN HIS final prayer for His followers revealed that He came to earth for *three* main reasons.

First, He came to reveal His and our Father to the world. Jesus and His Father are one, united in purpose. They share the same desire for the salvation of the entire world.

Second, Jesus came to earth to reveal to us how we can be reconciled and reunited with His Father. He showed us how we can have fellowship with Him, how we can commune with Him. This we accomplish through daily, unhurried prayer. Prayer as we have seen is spending unhurried time with God. Our Father is eager to be close to us.

Third, Jesus came to earth to die for the sins of the world. He came to reconcile to the Father those who would accept His sacrifice.

This prayer was specific for His disciples. While Jesus was around, they were safe. Only one turned from Jesus: Judas, and the devil took control of him. It is possible to know about Jesus, and yet, not have a saving relationship with him.

It is instructive that on the night Jesus was betrayed, He

was praying with and for His disciples. But Judas was not present during this time of prayer. John records:

> When He had finished praying, Jesus left with His disciples and crossed the Kidron Valley. On the other side there was a garden, and He and His disciples went into it.
>
> Now Judas, who betrayed Him, knew the place, because Jesus had often met there with His disciples. So Judas came to the garden, guiding a detachment of soldiers and some officials from the chief priests and the Pharisees. They were carrying torches, lanterns and weapons. (John 18:1-3)

The eleven had the privilege to hear their Master pray for them. He prayed that they may experience his joy. Life with all its anxieties should not rob them of the joy that a relationship with the Savior brings. A joyful Christian life can be experienced in this world of sin and evil. As the saying goes, "Don't let the devil steal your joy." This joy can be maintained only by those who keep in daily contact with Jesus through prayer.

To be casual about the daily practice of prayer can be fatal. It is important that our lives be surrendered to God daily. John, a few chapters earlier, reveals something shockingly strange about Judas that should make us take note. Jesus washed Judas' feet and then shared the passover meal with him. But John writes, "As soon as Judas took the bread, Satan entered into him. So Jesus told him, "What you are about to do, do quickly" (John 13:27).

How could the devil take control of Judas while he was in the very presence of Jesus? Again, we can learn that it is not enough to know about Jesus or even talk about Him. It is vitally important that our lives are surrendered to Him, and this we do through daily, sincere prayer.

The devil does not care how much we know about Jesus; he is ready to take control of our lives if we are not experiencing, daily, a close relationship with God. Through daily prayer, we can claim the answer to Jesus' prayer for us. He prayed for our protection from the "evil one."

However, this prayer is not for the world He came to save, but for His close followers only, those who accepted Him and His Father whom He came to reveal. His departure was imminent—that very night He would be betrayed, arrested, and would soon die. He was preparing His close friends for this ordeal. They would be left in a sinful and dangerous world. He therefore prayed for His Father's protection over them; He wanted them to know that they would not be alone. Heaven's protection would always be present.

Jesus also prayed that they be sanctified. To be sanctified is to be set apart or to be made holy. How would this be done? It would be done by the truth, the Word of God. The child of God, for whom Jesus prayed, will be attracted to the Word of God. He becomes a student of God's Word, and through prayer and study of God's Word experiences God's life-changing power.

Questions for Reflection

1) What are the three main reasons Jesus came to earth?

2) For what blessings did Jesus pray for His disciples?

3) What confidence is renewed each day as we prayerfully commune with our heavenly Father?

Prayer

Heavenly Father, I thank You that Jesus came to earth to reveal who You are. He also came to assure us that we are not left alone in this evil world. Now protect me from the "evil one." Embrace me with the love You shared with Jesus, Your sinless Son. May the day come quickly when I will be with You in glory. Come quickly Lord Jesus, come. Amen.

Lesson 23

Prayer and the Mission of Jesus, Part 2

John 17:20-25

"My prayer is not for them alone. I pray also for those who will believe in Me through their message, that all of them may be one, Father, just as You are in Me and I am in You. May they also be in Us so that the world may believe that You have sent Me. I have given them the glory that You gave Me, that they may be one as We are one: I in them and You in me. May they be brought to complete unity to let the world know that You sent Me and have loved them even as You have loved Me. Father, I want those You have given Me to be with Me where I am, and to see My glory, the glory You have given Me because You loved Me before the creation of the world. "Righteous Father, though the world does not know You, I know You, and they know that You have sent Me. I have made You known to them, and will continue to make You known in order that the love You have for Me may be in them and that I Myself may be in them."

JESUS DID NOT pray for His disciples alone—He prayed for another group, too. The Savior prayed for those who would believe in Him because of the disciples' witness. For all who accept His death for their sins, Jesus prayed this final prayer. He reveals in this prayer that they belong not only to Him, but to His father also. You are included in that prayer. *Jesus prayed for you!*

Because we have accepted the sacrifice of Jesus and are reconciled to His Father, when we pray, we can claim the answers to this prayer of Jesus. He prayed for our protection in this evil world, and it is our privilege to claim that protection each day when we pray. But what protection do we need? Jesus prayed that we be protected from the "evil one," the devil. What He prayed for His disciples, He also prayed for us. We can claim that protection daily when we pray. We can, each day, as we commune with our heavenly Father, know that the devil has no power over us. We are protected as long as we fellowship and converse with our Father in heaven.

Jesus also prayed that all of us who accept Him and are reunited with His Father be also united with each other. We are God's children whose desire is to grow closer to Him, and the closer we are drawn to Him, the closer we are drawn to each other. This is achieved as we daily fellowship with the Father through prayer. John says, "No one has ever seen God; but if we love one another, God lives in us and his love is made complete in us" (1John 4:12). The more we pray to our heavenly Father, the greater is our desire and ability to love each other.

Our Savior prayed that we experience the same love He

and His Father share. We can claim that unique love daily through prayer. It is our privilege to know, as John says: "See what great love the Father has lavished on us, that we should be called children of God! And that is what we are!" (1 John 3:1).

Jesus also prayed that we would be with Him in glory, in heaven where He is, in the presence of His Father. We can wait for that day with confidence when we will ascend into heaven and be with the Lord. This confidence is renewed each day as we fellowship with our Father and our Savior in prayer. What hope and assurance is our privilege to experience each day! This is the joy and excitement of prayer. It places us in the very atmosphere of heaven, while we tarry in this world of sin and evil.

Jesus prayed that we be in Him and His Father, that the world may know that His Father sent Him. Being in Him means knowing Him intimately, and this is achieved only through daily contact with Him through prayer. The Savior also prayed that we experience the same love His Father had for Him and that the world knows that we are experiencing His divine love. How awesome! People should be able to see that God loves us!

That's how important prayer is, for it keeps us in close fellowship with God. Each day we are telling others that we know God and that He loves us, or we are revealing that we do not know Him and His love. Our lives are to be a testimony each day of the love of God. Wherever we are, in our homes, on our jobs, in the community, or in church, our lives should display the love of God. Prayer makes this possible, for it keeps us in tune with God who is love.

Questions for Reflection

1) How can we be assured that the devil has no power over us?

2) Is your life a revelation of God's love each day? If not, how can it be?

3) Jesus prayed that we be with Him in glory. How can we keep that hope alive?

Prayer

Thank you, Lord Jesus, that You prayed for me. Draw me close to You and fill my heart with Your love, that it may overflow to others. Grant me that oneness with You and the Father for which You prayed. I long to be with You in glory. Keep me trusting in You till that blessed day, I pray. Amen.

HEAVEN'S RESPONSE TO PRAYER

LUKE 3:21, 22

When all the people were being baptized, Jesus was baptized too. And as He was praying, heaven was opened and the Holy Spirit descended on Him in bodily form like a dove. And a voice came from heaven: "You are my Son, whom I love; with You I am well pleased."

JESUS WAS BAPTIZED by John the Baptist. This marked the beginning of His public ministry. For about thirty years He was preparing for this mission of teaching, healing, and revealing His Father. Now the time had come, and Jesus bowed in prayer; He would first commune with His Father in heaven.

Jesus would not attempt this work of saving sinners and revealing His Father on His own. He called to heaven in prayer for strength and support. He would not begin without His Father's blessing and approval.

What was the response from heaven? A corridor from heaven to earth opened, and the Holy Spirit took on the form of a dove and journeyed down this heavenly corridor and rested on Jesus as He prayed. The Father then spoke from heaven, "You are my Son, whom I love; with You I am well pleased."

Here Jesus teaches us, by example, that success in the mission of proclaiming the Gospel to the world needs heaven's approval and power. We too, need to await the power of the Holy Spirit and listen for God's voice of commendation before we attempt preaching to others. Through prayer, like Jesus did, we can receive heaven's approval and heaven's power.

When we seek God's blessing through prayer for the accomplishing of His mission to save sinners, we can be assured that as it was for Jesus, so it will be for us. Heaven will pour out its blessings, the Holy Spirit will empower our lives, and God will speak to our hearts. We will be strengthened by our heavenly Father's assurance: "You are my son or daughter, with you I am well pleased." Then we can confidently witness for Jesus and rejoice as He saves all who accept Him.

Questions for Reflection

1) What did Jesus do after His baptism and before He began His public ministry?

2) How did heaven respond to the prayer of Jesus?

3) What important lesson was Jesus teaching by turning to His Father through prayer?

Prayer

Loving Lord, help me to turn to You before I attempt anything for You or for others. Assure me first that You are pleased with me. Help me to learn the true source of all success. Pour out Your Holy Spirit into my life, that I may do Your will. Grant me these blessings in the name of my Lord and Savior, Jesus Christ. Amen.

Lesson 25

Praying Like Jesus

Luke 23:34

Jesus said, "Father, forgive them, for they do not know what they are doing...."

The gospels record three prayers of Jesus on the cross. Surely, Jesus was in constant communion and fellowship with His Father as He paid the ultimate price and made the amazing sacrifice for our sins. The life of Jesus was bathed in prayer. Prayer was a daily experience, and though He could not at that time escape to a lonely place to commune with His Father, He still held His private audience with heaven.

Here Jesus prayed the most selfless prayer that can ever be prayed. He prayed not for Himself, though He was in agony—no! He prayed for those who crucified Him:

"Father, forgive them, for they do not know what they are doing."

Did they not know what they were doing? They were killing Him. But Jesus, through prayer, looked deeper into their souls. They did not know the power, the Devil, the real enemy who worked through them. They did not know God, and the devil took charge of their lives.

Jesus by example, under this most extreme test, teaches us that prayer is not a selfish act. He prayed for those who crucified Him, those who did not deserve nor sought His forgiveness. He was practicing what He taught in His first teaching on prayer: "Love your enemies, bless those who curse you, do good to those who hate you and pray for those who persecute you" (Luke 6:27, 28).

Could it be that our attitude towards radical Muslims or murderous criminals is an indication that we are not children of God, though we profess to be Christians? Nothing proves more clearly that we are sons and daughters of God than praying for the forgiveness and the redemption of those who persecute us, those who act as our enemies. The comment by one leader of the National Rifle Association, in response to Adam Lanza fatally shooting twenty children and six adult staff members at *Sandy Hook Elementary School,* that "the only protection from a bad guy with a gun is a good guy with a gun," is woefully shortsighted and certainly an un-Christlike statement. The Christian way can never be survival by the best armed. How sad that in 20 States, concealed guns are allowed in church!

Communion and fellowship with God results in an

amazing change, a complete transformation of our lives—we become more concerned for others than ourselves. We know that we are safe in God's hands, even in the face of death, and our greater desire and concern is for those who do not know our Savior and Lord. We do not pray for retribution—we pray for their redemption. Like Jesus, we realize that those who would do us wrong do not know what they're doing. They do not know the God who loves them and longs to fellowship with them and transform their lives.

It is our privilege to pray as Jesus did, but this can be our experience only as we daily commune with our God in prayer. Then are we truly sons and daughters of our Father in heaven, for our lives become reflections of His perfect, loving, and forgiving character.

Questions for Reflection

1) How will you describe this prayer of Jesus on the cross?

2) What significant lesson did Jesus teach through this prayer on the cross?

3) What attitude will those who truly pray have toward those who do them harm?

Prayer

O Lord, give me the grace that Jesus demonstrated on the cross. Teach me to pray for those who do me wrong. Help me never to forget that I need Your forgiveness just as much as they do. Change me, O God, that I may be more concerned about others than myself. Because I know You, I can entrust my life into Your care and plead for those who do not know You. Teach me to pray as Jesus did. Amen.

CHURCH— A HOUSE OF PRAYER

Matthew 21:12, 13

Jesus entered the temple courts and drove out all who were buying and selling there. He overturned the tables of the money changers and the benches of those selling doves. "It is written," He said to them, "'My house will be called a house of prayer,' but you are making it 'a den of robbers.'"

Why do we go to church? Do we have a clear understanding of the purpose of worship?

When Jesus was on earth, the purpose of worship was terribly misunderstood. The temple, the place of worship, was full of activity—money-making activity. The reason for worship faded as the people argued and jostled over the price of the sacrificial animals that were to represent the coming Savior.

Jesus was saddened by this utter disregard for the place

of worship. He intervened by overturning the tables of the money traders and animal sellers, and declared, "It is written, 'My house will be called a house of prayer.'"

Could it be that we today also miss the real purpose of worship? Jesus says the place of worship is a place of prayer. Since prayer is communion with God, church therefore should be the place where worshipers gather to commune with God. The place of worship is a place of encounter, a place we meet with Jesus and our heavenly Father. It is a place of prayer.

Wherever and whenever we meet together for worship, we should leave changed, transformed because we communed with the great God of heaven. To talk with God, to listen for and hear His voice, is a life-changing experience. Do we have such an encounter when we worship?

Worship is not for entertainment or for show. It is not about great programming or style of worship. Should we leave worship unchanged, our meeting, no matter how grand or solemn, is of no spiritual benefit. All singing, preaching, and praying should have one primary goal: to lead each worshiper to experience an encounter with Jesus our Savior and fellowship with our Father in heaven.

We should therefore come to the place of worship, the church, with an attitude of prayer. Church attendance is not necessarily worship unless we experience an encounter with Jesus our Savior who longs to reveal to us the loving heart of His Father who sent Him to redeem us.

Questions for Reflection

1) Why do you go to church?

2) What should be our focus when we go to the place of worship?

3) How can we avoid attending church and leaving without an encounter with God?

Prayer

Heavenly Father, thank You for this revelation Jesus gave about worship. Please forgive and teach me to focus on You whenever I go to the place of worship. May I come before You always with an attitude of prayer, seeking communion with You and my Savior, Jesus. Grant me the transformed life I need whenever I meet in Your house for worship. This I humbly pray in Your Son's blessed name. Amen.

Lesson 27

A STRANGE PRAYER

Matthew 27:46

About the ninth hour Jesus cried out in a loud voice, "Eloi, Eloi, lama sabachthani?"—which means, "My God, my God, why have you forsaken me?"

The second prayer of Jesus on the cross is the strangest prayer He ever prayed, and it seems contradictory to His other prayers. He prayed, "My God, my God, why have you forsaken me?"

How could Jesus pray such of prayer when He was in regular communion and a fellowship with His Father? Did He forget that His Father loved Him and would never forsake Him? Did He forget that He and His Father are one? Did He forget the voice of His Father when He twice spoke, "You are my son, whom I love, with you I am well pleased?" *No, He did not forget.*

Sin is so offensive to God that as our Savior hung on the cross, bearing our guilt, He felt His Father had abandoned Him. He could not at that moment share communion and fellowship with His Father as They did before. Jesus was experiencing the cost, the penalty of sin. How could His Father hold communion and fellowship with Him as He bore the sin of the world? Sin, for a moment, it would seem, blocked His view of His Father's presence. He felt forsaken and alone.

Thank Jesus, He bore our sins that we need not feel forsaken! Our heavenly Father always welcomes us into His holy presence because our Savior, Jesus Christ, felt the separation from Him that sin causes. Jesus experienced it in our behalf. We can now come boldly, with confidence before a holy God, with full assurance that He will never forsake us.

When we come into His presence, as is our privilege through prayer each day, our Father will say of us as He said of Jesus, "You are my son, you are my daughter, whom I love; with you I am well pleased." It is our privilege to experience through daily communion with God through prayer, what He promised as recorded by David, "Though my father and mother forsake me, the LORD will receive me" (Psalm 27:10).

Questions for Reflection

1) Why does this prayer of Jesus seem strange and out of character?

2) What does the example of Jesus teach us we should do when we feel forsaken and alone?

3) What does the aloneness Jesus felt teach us about the way God views sin and our need to confess our sins in prayer?

Prayer

Lord Jesus, I praise You for accepting my sins and bearing the rejection I deserve. Help me to recognize how offensive sin is to a holy God. Let me never cherish evil but turn to You in repentance and receive Your cleansing. Oh Father, thank You for receiving me because Jesus died in my place. Amen.

Lesson 28

PRAYER— A SHOUT OF VICTORY

John 19:28-30

Later, knowing that everything had now been finished, and so that Scripture would be fulfilled, Jesus said, "I am thirsty." A jar of wine vinegar was there, so they soaked a sponge in it, put the sponge on a stalk of the hyssop plant, and lifted it to Jesus' lips. When He had received the drink, Jesus said, "It is finished." With that, He bowed His head and gave up His spirit.

SINCE THE DAY Adam and Eve sinned, a conflict, a battle over the fate of men has raged. The devil's determination to destroy man has never ceased. Even the people selected by God to preserve His name and way of life had turned from Him. The Jews rejected and crucified the One who came to save them, the One who came to reveal the true character of the God they claimed to follow. The devil had succeeded in corrupting even their worship, which became mere tradition and formality.

On the cross, the Savior hung representing the evil of sin, its unchecked brutality. Man had descended to such evil that they thought doing such cruelty, crucifying an innocent man, gave glory and honor to God.

Jesus bore the agony and pain with such dignity. He even demonstrated the forgiving and saving heart of God as He promised the thief on the cross, "You will be with Me in paradise." Jesus would demonstrate that even while dying, He was still in control and had power to save. This marvelous, matchless, saving grace of God, the Devil could never defeat.

Our Savior knew that the purpose for which He left heaven to come to earth was now complete. The Devil's ultimate evil display, the Crucifixion, was in reality God's sacrificial act. Jesus did reveal that He had power to lay His life down and take it up again. Dying on the cross was His signal that the Devil and sin will finally be defeated. The price for man's redemption was paid. His death signaled that through Him, we can be victorious over the devil and sin. "It is finished!" was His victorious shout.

Those words of triumph should inspire us when we pray. Through prayer we call to a Savior who has finished His work of saving us. He has finished the fight against the Devil for us. Our fight, then, is not against the Devil but is the "fight of faith," the fight to trust Jesus who defeated the Devil and won the battle for us.

Prayer is therefore the acceptance of the finished work

of Jesus for us. It is the recognition that through Jesus Christ, we are more than conquerors over the devil and sin. Sin no longer holds dominion over us. When we pray, our hearts can be filled with joy, for like the dying thief on the cross, we too will be with our Lord in paradise.

Thank Jesus for His shout of victory, *"It is finished"*!

Questions for Reflection

1) What does the cross reveal about the nature of man?

2) The crucifixion of Jesus was the Devil's ultimate display of evil, but what does it reveal about God?

3) What was Jesus revealing when He declared, "It is finished"?

Prayer

O Jesus, my Savior, I praise You for dying in my place. Thank You for Your triumphant words, "It is finished!" that inspire me with hope. Draw me into a trusting relationship with You. I accept You as my Lord and ask that You live Your victorious life through me each day. For this I pray. Amen.

A PRAYER OF TRUST

LUKE 23:46

Jesus called out with a loud voice, "Father, into Your hands I commit my spirit." When He had said this, He breathed His last.

JESUS HAD JUST cried out, "My God, my God, why have You forsaken Me?" He had felt shut out from the presence and fellowship He enjoyed with His Father throughout His ministry. Sin had caused Him to feel alone and abandoned. The oneness He had enjoyed with His Father seemed broken as He bore the curse of sin.

However, Jesus knew His Father, and though He felt alone, He knew He could still trust Him. The sins of the world that He bore, though offensive and revolting to His Father, could not break His trust and confidence in Him.

Jesus knew that just as He felt alone, His Father also felt alone.

As the heavy weight of our sins crushed the life out of our Savior, He prayed His final prayer on the cross: "Father, into Your hand I commit My spirit." Jesus was praying, "Father, I trusted You in life, I will trust You in death. Yes, I feel alone because sin is so offensive to Your holy nature, but I know You, My Father, so well, that I still trust You. Death cannot separate me from Your love."

Jesus had "power to lay His life down and take it up again," but He committed His life into His Father's care.

Death is the common but cruel experience we all share as the inevitable consequence of sin. Jesus, through this prayer, teaches us how we can face this common enemy, death. When we trust our heavenly Father through life, we will also trust Him in death. When we learn to trust God through prayer each day, we will have no fear of death. We too can pray, "Father, into Your hand I commit My spirit," for nothing can separate us from God's love. Like Paul, we can shout, "...I am convinced that neither death nor life, neither angels nor demons, neither the present nor the future, nor any powers, neither height nor depth, nor anything else in all creation, will be able to separate us from the love of God that is in Christ Jesus our Lord" (Romans 8:38, 39).

Jesus experienced the separation from His Father that we should have experienced so that we can always feel loved and accepted by our heavenly Father. Nothing can ever separate us from His love. It is our privilege to be blessed in our Father's holy presence, daily, as we spend unhurried time in friendship and conversation with Him through prayer. Prayer is truly an experience of heaven while we are still here on this earth. *What a joyful privilege to be friends of God!*

Questions for Reflection

1) What does this final prayer of Jesus on the cross teach us about His trust in His father?

2) What can we learn from this prayer of Jesus about how we can face death?

3) What experience can we have through daily prayer?

Prayer

Heavenly Father, my life is in Your hands. Thank You for the promise that nothing can separate me from Your love, not even death. May this conviction grow as I come to You each day for fellowship and communion through prayer. Because of Jesus, who died for me, I need not fear death, for into Your hand I will commit myself. Bless me with this heavenly assurance, I pray. Amen.

Lesson 30

SEVEN CONVICTIONS YOU NEED WHEN YOU PRAY

Matthew 6:9-15

"This, then, is how you should pray:

'Our Father in heaven,
hallowed be Your name,
Your kingdom come,
Your will be done,
on earth as it is in heaven.
Give us today our daily bread.
And forgive us our debts,
as we also have forgiven our debtors.
And lead us not into temptation,
but deliver us from the evil one.'

"For if you forgive other people when they sin against you, your heavenly Father will also forgive you. But if you do not forgive others their sins, your Father will not forgive your sins."

In what we affectionately call the "Lord's prayer," Jesus revealed seven convictions we should have when we pray. He distinguishes this experience of prayer as distinctly different from the way the hypocrites and pagans pray. Let us take a closer look at this prayer.

Conviction #1

GOD IS MY FATHER
"Our Father"

- He loves me.
- He is responsible for me being born into this world.
- As a Father, He will protect and guide me, His child, if I let him.
- I can trust Him.
- I can share with Him my concerns and my needs.

Conviction #2

GOD DWELLS IN HEAVEN
"Our Father in heaven"

- He is in control of everything.
- He is beyond and above all.
- He is more than a Father: He is God Almighty who rules heaven and earth.

- All are subject to Him—angels, demons, and all who dwell in the earth.
- Yet as our Father, He chooses to be a personal God who responds to my needs.
- He answers prayer.

Conviction #3

GOD IS HOLY
"Hallowed be Your name"

- His name is holy.
- He deserves respect.
- We are privileged to approach Him each time we pray.
- We must come before Him with reverence and awe.
- We should come before Him, in prayer, recognizing we are sinners and He is holy and He is righteous.
- This recognition removes our pride and as a child we humbly seek His blessings.

Conviction #4

GOD'S RIGHTEOUS KINGDOM WILL COME
"Your kingdom come, Your will be done on earth as it is in heaven"

- We should pray for His righteous Kingdom to be established.
- We should pray for His righteous reign to be established on earth and sin be ended.
- Pray for His will to be done, first in your life, as it is done in heaven.
- Recognize that far more important than physical or material needs is the need for the will of God to be done on earth.
- God's supreme will is that we know Him and Jesus Christ, our Savior whom He sent that we may have eternal life.

Conviction #5

GOD PROVIDES FOR OUR DAILY NEEDS
"Give us this day our daily bread"

- God is aware of and will supply our daily needs.
- We can be confident that as a father provides for his child, so our God will provide for our needs.

- When He gives us more than we need, He's giving to us opportunities and blessings to meet the needs of others.
- It is a selfish heart that stores up more than it needs while closing its eyes to the needs of others.
- God has provided abundantly and sufficiently for the daily needs of all, but selfishness has caused some to become wealthy while others die for lack of food.
- The fact there are billionaires and millionaires in our world, while others are dying of hunger anywhere in our world, is a betrayal of the prayer Jesus taught us to pray.
- The "free market" system, the "American dream" philosophy, is based on selfishness and greed and is not consistent with the "Lord's Prayer."
- To pray "Our Father" is a reminder that we are our brother's keeper, and God provides for the daily needs of all His children through the generosity of those who are blessed by Him.
- When God uses us to meet the daily needs of others, we are helping them to recognize their most important need, their need of God.

- Jesus reminds us that it is hard for a rich man to enter the kingdom (Matthew 19:23, 24).
- The poor pray for their daily needs, the rich often pay others to supply their daily needs and are in danger of trusting in their abundance, instead of God.
- God's principle for those who pray to Him is, "Give, and it will be given to you…" (Luke 6:38).

CONVICTION #6

GOD FORGIVES AND ENABLES US TO ALSO FORGIVE

"Forgive us our debts as we have forgiven our debtors"

- We all debtors, sinners.
- We all owe somebody something, and anything we owe anyone, we owe to God, for we are all children of God.
- Anytime we sin against someone, we also sin against God, for each of us is a child of God.
- Anything I do that is not a loving act is a debt I owe to God and man.
- Anything I do that is harmful to anyone, in word or deed, is a sin against God that needs forgiveness.

- Consistent with the way Jesus taught us to pray is Paul's advice, "Let no debt remain outstanding, except the continuing debt to love one another, for he who loves his fellow man has fulfilled the law" (Romans 13:8).
- Jesus concluded, if you will not forgive those who sin against you, God will not forgive you.
- A person who receives God's forgiveness becomes forgiving.

Conviction #7

GOD PROTECTS

"...and lead us not into temptation but deliver us from the evil one"

- Temptations are always around us.
- This sinful world, this vile world, is not a "friend of grace" as the hymn writer, Isaac Watts, says.
- Jesus reminds us that the devil is the ruler of this world; He calls him the "Prince of this world" (John 12:31; John 14:30; John 16:11).
- God will guide us away from situations and circumstances that can cause us to be tempted to turn from Him; for that we should pray.

- We can claim the promise, "God is faithful; He will not let you be tempted beyond what you can bear. But when you are tempted, he will provide a way out so that you can stand up under it" (1 Corinthians 10:13).
- We should not trust our own strength or be overconfident about our spiritual strength. We should humbly trust in God's strength and wisdom daily.
- Every day it is our privilege to trust, to depend on our heavenly Father for victory over the devil and his temptations.
- The evil one, the Devil, knows our weaknesses; he knows what temptation will overcome us when we are out of God's protection. We must therefore remain under our Father's careful watch through prayer.

Prayer is our joyful privilege, when we learn to pray as Jesus taught. Every area of our lives is under our Father's watchful care. Thank God we are never left to face the Devil's assaults in this hostile world alone! Through prayer, our heavenly Father is always with us.

Lord, teach us to pray.